THE
SOBER
ALTRUIST

A HUMANIST
MOTIVATING
PHILOSOPHY

THE
SOBER
ALTRUIST

A HUMANIST
MOTIVATING
PHILOSOPHY

VINCENT P. BURKHARDT

VPB PRESS

The Sober Altruist: *A Humanist Motivating Philosophy*

Published by VPB Press
Denver, Colorado, U.S.A.

BURKHARDT, VINCENT P., Author
THE SOBER ALTRUIST
VINCENT P. BURKHARDT

Library of Congress Control Number: 2023920420

ISBN: 979-8-9893596-0-8, 979-8-9893596-1-5 (paperback)
ISBN: 979-8-9893596-2-2 (digital)

PHILOSOPHY / Movements / Humanism
EDUCATION / Philosophy, Theory & Social Aspects
SOCIAL SCIENCE / Activism & Social Justice

Publishing Management: Susie Schaefer (FinishTheBookPublishing.com)

QUANTITY PURCHASES: Schools, companies, professional groups, clubs, and other organizations may qualify for special terms when ordering quantities of this title. For information, email thesoberaltruist@gmail.com.

TABLE OF CONTENTS

so·ber

serious, sensible, and solemn[21]

al·tru·ist

an unselfish person whose actions show concern for the welfare of others[22]

an animal that behaves in a way that is not beneficial to or may be harmful to itself, but which benefits the survival of others of its species[22]

INTRODUCTION

҂

The human experience has always been one of constant change; powers shift, rulers die, economies crash, and cultures evolve. The pace at which this change happens is not set, nor is there any promise that this change will move humanity in a positive direction. It is easy to step outside your front door and watch people live their lives in our modern era and assume that what you are witnessing is normal; it is not. It merely masquerades as such because it is a validation of your experiences in your place and time. Our moment in history could not be less normal, less different from the experiences of those who have come before. Of course, there are elements of our world, such as food, family, language, and conflict, that have always been constants of the human condition, but the historically recent industrialization of our world has presented humanity with innumerable and novel conditions, opportunities, and risks.

Perhaps the most obvious modification to the human experience in the last one hundred years has been the pace of change, largely catalyzed by rapid technological advance. Let's take transportation as a quick example. Humans have been using horses as their primary means of transport[1] (where

geographically available) for nearly five thousand years—
that is a five-thousand-year period during which something
better than a horse was not created, and land transportation
technologies barely evolved. The first production model of a
car began in 1886[2], 137 years before this book. In those 137
years, we have seen the proliferation of automobiles change
the very face of our cities and even cultures and witnessed
the rise of electric cars and massive global logistics systems
largely predicated on the use of automobiles. In addition, we
have seen aviation technology go from a pipe dream to the
Boeing 737 and the internet evolve from a military curiosity to
a global platform reshaping human societies. Of course, over
those same 137 years, we also created the means of our own
nuclear self-annihilation. Do not be fooled. We do not live in
ordinary times. We do not live in a world where we use the
same technologies our great-great-grandfathers did, let alone
use the same technologies we ourselves did even five years
ago. We don't just live in interesting times, we live in unprecedented ones.

While sprinting as we are toward the technological and
civilizational unknown, there is a part of us that has lagged
woefully behind. Civilizations are only as wise as the values
and ideals that guide them, whether their emphasis is placed
on profit, competition, and cognitive predation or the supplica-
tion of effort toward protecting individual freedoms, beauty,
and a commitment to the human future. In this age, we are
given the means to master our world, and yet, we so often
choose to wield our newfound might without aim or guiding
principles. There has never been a time in human history when
what we choose to believe and the values we hold will more
completely determine the shape of the human future simply

because our ability to shape that future has never been more profound. The promise of humanity in our age is either a future filled with freedom, prosperity, and even cosmic proliferation or servitude, greed, and the deconstruction of the very things that make us human. What, then, are the values and ideals that might keep us from our darkest promise?

Here is a truth equally as freeing as it is damming and inseparable from the conditions of modern man: There is no absolute, immutable, inescapable value structure under which we all must heel. No absolute value or meaning exists beyond that which man creates and chooses. Even religion, systems of being, and schemas of reality that expressly profess to possess the absolute truth must be chosen and accepted into the hearts of men for them to become absolute, and even then, only so for those who have chosen them. Ultimately, you the individual are responsible for the philosophies, values, truths, and motives you allow to inform the course and conditions of your own life, but unlike the ephemeral beliefs that may have spawned them, the consequences of your chosen mode of being are observable and absolute. We choose what we make of ourselves, and in so doing, we shape our world.

This book presents the basics of a value structure, a motivating philosophy rooted in the existential realities of the human story and the necessary obligations we all must hold toward its continuity and prosperity. Sober Altruism, which is explained within this book, is fundamentally a Humanist ideology, a system of ideas strung together to facilitate an individual's choice to serve the species, to stand vigil over our future and choose a life of meaning and consequence even if that choice does not promise comfort, ease, or the absolute truths of the universe.

Herein is the fundamental aim of Sober Altruism, to separate apathy from action and moral relativity from the advancement of Humankind and the defense of our Existential Liberties.

IN DEFENSE OF IDEOLOGY, THE HEURISTICS OF LIFE

⁕

Ideology exists among those quietly tabooed concepts of the twenty-first century as traditionalism or faith. These concepts bring with them histories spanning nearly our entire existence and include the good but also, of course, the appalling. The contemporary origins of the modern distaste for ideology can be traced to many sources, but perhaps one of the more significant is the postmodernist movements[3, 4] in the wake of World Wars One and Two. This aversion is not difficult to understand; certain ideologies lit the newly industrialized world ablaze twice in a period of less than thirty-five years only to be followed by numerous smaller conflicts (many of which continue to this day) and the potential for nuclear apocalypse again, largely catalyzed by certain ideologies both political and religious. What is often missed in this analysis, however, is the positive influence ideology can have on communities and individuals. The baby, so to speak, is often thrown out with the bathwater. Despite its obvious risks if taken to an extreme, ideology has always possessed inherent and essential utility to the human experience. This short chapter will challenge the absolutist phobia of ideology by exploring its benefits and reframing the topic into something more rational and more palatable to the modern ear.

First, what is ideology? Ideology is defined as "a system of ideas and ideals, especially one which forms the basis of economic or political theory and policy."[23] A system of ideas and ideals, that's all. There is no Communist bogeyman waiting in the words of this definition to radicalize the young innocent passersby nor Swastikas spinning behind the punctuation. Unless, of course, we put them there. Ideology is systemized and organized ideas, something we all (whether we call it ideology or not) build and use every day. Every opinion you share or stance you hold is predicated on one or numerous systems of ideas you have built inside your mind. Some people subscribe to shared systems of ideas; some do not. Some people have these systems of ideas highly ordered and articulated; others do not. While we can acknowledge that ideology is not without flaws and risks, we must also acknowledge that its constructive and positive qualities make it an important aspect of human society, and one that has likely existed as long as we have. Ideology provides a foundation for collective and individual identity, intellectual exploration, ethical deliberation, and social change, among more. We will briefly expand upon three of the most significant benefits of ideology, the first of which is perhaps the most valuable.

Temet Nosce (know thyself).

Ideology provides individuals with a sense of identity, a framework to better understand who they are, what they stand for, and how they should relate to others, themselves, and more generally, the world. While organized ideology is not essential to possessing certainty of self, it is a useful heuristic for individuals to explore and assert values and principles while also motivating action and informing lifestyle. Additionally, shared ideology provides numerous communal benefits such as a shared purpose and set of values, which helps foster a sense of solidarity and cohesion among like-minded individuals. Ideology has always been a driving force in the creation and cohesion of human communities[5]. As the influence of theistic ideologies wanes, there is less and less for communities to derive cohesion from, and individuals may find it easier to further atomize and separate themselves from their fellow man. Regardless of the elements binding human communities, they are absolute in their importance to human survival, prosperity, and happiness[5]. Whether communal or singular, ideology is to identity what an anvil is to a tool, a mechanism that helps guide how we shape ourselves.

The second fundamental benefit of ideology is in providing a framework for analysis, adjudication, and action. Ideology provides a lens through which we can analyze and interpret complex social, political, and economic issues. It offers a structured way of understanding the world, allowing us to make sense of events and phenomena, identify patterns, and draw conclusions. This analytical framework can help us navigate the complexities of our society and inform our decision-making processes even and maybe, especially, in environments saturated with information and manipulative bias. A concrete position is a powerful tool in rooting and motivating the individual to a moral direction. Appreciating the value of judgment, the arbitration of the truth from lies, or the good from the malicious or malign is a blade upon which civilizations have always rested. A person unable to stand with truth and goodness or even unable to identify these things is a person who can be blown by the political winds to whatever ends, whatever definitions of good and true are most convenient to those currently in power. In ideology's provision of a stance, it endows individuals and communities with internal normative guidance by outlining a set of values and principles that help guide and filter external ethical judgments, positions, and actions. Ideology provides a moral compass, helping us determine what is right and wrong, just and unjust, and desirable and undesirable. Ultimately, ideology can help insulate individuals from moral drift even if the culture and politics of their host society degenerate around them.

Perhaps equal in its importance to identity is ideological expression as a purpose and a catalyst for action. Ideology can be and has been a driving force behind many social, political, and cultural transformations across the ages. It inspires individuals and communities to challenge the status quo, advocate for change, and strive for a better future. By promoting certain ideals and goals, ideology can mobilize collective action, spark movements, and drive societal progress. There are few greater changes you can make in a society than to change how that society and those within systematize and organize ideas. The mobilization of will and effort toward well-articulated ends with solid foundations rooted in a shared system of ideas has always had the power to change the trajectory of the human future. Though these collective manifestations of mobilized ideology are potentially world-altering, what's more essential to note is the effect it can have on individuals. While you may not die from fecklessness or a meaningless life, you will suffer, bleed, and cry, and everyone you love will eventually die, not because   you did not believe in something, but because that is the way of life for all of us. The question then becomes, why do we suffer and yet persist? What is the reason you choose to endure? What is your purpose? Ideology has always been the salve to settle these uncomfortable questions and sharpen people toward a purpose, a reason to endure even in the darkest of times.

Ideology is foremost a mechanism through which we can find our place, identity, community, and, of course, purpose. The experience of sentients is a million maddening questions wrapped up into one big, beautiful enigma, and ideologies are the heuristics we use to make sense of that question from our limited perspective of the infinity that surrounds us. We cannot see all things from all angles nor predict the future with any degree of certainty, and so, in the absence of that omnipotence, we are left with only good intent and heuristics. This is the ultimate role and value of ideology, to serve as our heuristics of life, the means through which we can systematize and simplify the infinite and unknowable such that we can operate in our world with meaning, impact, and direction.

THE SEVEN FOUNDATIONS
OF THE SOBER ALTRUIST

$$\ast$$

Sober Altruism, or "SobAlt" as we'll frequently call it from here on for the sake of brevity, is foremost a Humanist ideology, a value structure aimed at protecting the human condition and its future. While other modes of Humanism exist, they are often mired by a poorly hidden disdain for the spiritual or weakened by a lack of articulated belief and cause. The insubstantial and often politically acquiescent nature of contemporary Humanism is not an insignificant motive for writing this book. When someone claims to be Christian, you know, at least, some of what that person believes and their values, largely regardless of who that person is. The moniker "Christian" has a defined and understood meaning. When someone claims to be a Humanist, there is no common understanding of the label that will ensure the moniker conveys anything beyond the most superficial. One of the more common and egregious rationalizations for adopting this title is some version of, "I am Humanist because I believe in people"; this means nothing, it is not a stance, nor can it inform a value structure. While there are examples of famous Humanists and Humanist organizations with more robust philosophies than the example above[6], they frequently have divergent definitions of what the title even means and what values it entails, if they present a value structure at all. To be clear, the aim of this book is not to unify Humanism or solve its many failings. It is to present a distinct genre of Humanism in a fashion that does provide concrete positions and value structures, free of the wispy relativism and impressionable dogmas that now hinder Humanism's necessary entrance into the global Zeitgeist. Following this brief critique, there seems to be no better place to start our exploration of SobAlt and its positions than with the core values and assertions that root the doctrine, of which there are seven.

First, SobAlt is a choice to adhere to a set of values that prioritizes humans and humanity. It is not some mawkish or mystical declaration of a "belief in people" but a sober recognition that we are in total a species like any other, subject to the same whims and malice of each other and our environment but if not for the labors of our progenitors and the capacities of our minds. Foremost, SobAlt is a choice, a personal declaration of value and priority.

Second, though the choice to prioritize species motivates the desire for altruism, an unarticulated desire to do good toward any end is insufficient and even hazardous. There are few regimes in history that persecuted great evil that did not believe they were doing what was right. "I want to do good" is an insufficient statement for optimistic morons incapable of imagining the dangers of ambiguity. A definition of what furthers the good of our species is thus necessary to create a coherent articulation and practice of Humanism.

Third, what is it that separates the new man from the old? The rich from the poor? The freed from the slave? In our long history, we have ever been the subject of existential bondage, the forced will of nature and tyrannies upon our lives. When the food walked away, we left our homes to follow; when sickness descended as plague, we died or worse, lived to see those whom we loved pass under the yolk of a hostile and unforgiving reality. Nobody chooses to be thrown into the world. Otherwise, none of us would elect to be born in times of subjection to disaster, deepest privation, or bondage. Yet for the lucky among us, those who reside in the modern, established world, we are freed from so much of the tides of unwanted dictations upon our lives. When we cut ourselves, we no longer die from infection; when we drink water, we no longer worry about cholera; and when we leave our homes and come back, they are still warm. All this we take for granted, forgetting that the lives we have been gifted are comfortable only because untold generations have built upon each other to give us this, a greater degree of freedom from the destructiveness and entropy of our world. So, I ask again, what separates the new man from the old? The rich from the poor? The freed from the slave? It is Existential Liberty, the degree with which a person or peoples possess the capacity to dictate the conditions and course of their existence. That is what is good. That constitutes human advance and is the beacon for the sober and true altruist, not to hoist burdens or conditions upon others but to work to expand their Existential Liberties, to give humanity the ability to write its own stories and bestow upon humans the gift of greater self-determination. The next chapter is solely dedicated to further qualifying Human Existential Liberty as the central value of SobAlt.

Four, the trajectory of our liberation from existential bondage is not linear; we can, we have, and we will fail to maintain what others have fought so hard to create and keep. It only takes one particularly lethal plague, one nuke, or one solar flare, and it's over. Our progress could be reset. All the sacrifice, work, blood, and pain undone, and if then, our dead could see us, they would weep. This reality constitutes the responsibility of the true altruist, to stand vigil, protect what we have, and fight for what we need; it is to acknowledge existential risks and the consequences of succumbing. Human Existential Liberties cannot be made in the absence of human continuity and the securities of continued existence.

Five, Human Primacy. We may not forsake all else on a whim, but we must be willing to forsake all else on the altar of human continuity and interest. Human Primacy is a necessary value that sets the priority of the true altruist. It is to put human interest above all else save perhaps for the essential transcendence of value itself. Human Primacy can best be understood in this perhaps crude parable: None should fell a tree out of boredom or malice, but we would burn a forest to ash to keep our children warm.

Six, the limitations and necessities of rationalism and science. The cult of science rises to replace the cult of myth, and yet science is only a tool, a mechanism of understanding the nature of reality and our relationship to it, but as incapable of illuminating a transcendent purpose as a hammer is incapable of writing a sonnet. Rationalism has given us a foundation upon which we blunt so many of the horrid dictations of reality, but rationalism and science cannot give us purpose. The more we learn of self, species, future, and environment, the better able we are to free ourselves from their bondage and the better we may pursue our purpose; this is the tool made masterpiece, the hammer held upon the nail, the vital utility of science and rationalism.

Seven, the gift of choosing true altruism is foremost one of responsibility. For those who accept the priority of species, the goodness of Existential Liberty, and the assertion of Human Primacy, there is given no comfort, no rosy lens upon the visage of reality. What is given is purpose alone, a conviction upon which to reassess our relationship with our future, our communities, our technology, and foremost, ourselves.

The rest of this book will serve as a means to expand upon this ideological frame and explore its most essential implications. There is no promise made that the words that follow will demystify the great questions of our reality as we all must seek these answers for ourselves and should do so, wherever they might come in the secular or spiritual. What this ideology does offer is this: SobAlt is an articulation of our existential realities such that we can best apply ourselves to the human endeavor and derive meaning and direction from it. SobAlt offers responsibility and purpose alone.

This, the enormous responsibility of being, to exist for a lifetime at the single point of human influence over the future, to be felt as long as humanity should endure, in misery or majesty.

A DEFINITION OF GOOD,
HUMAN EXISTENTIAL LIBERTY

$$\gtrless$$

As established in the previous chapter, the desire toward altruism must be tempered and shaped by a definition, an articulation of what constitutes human advance, of what, for our purposes at least, constitutes good for human individuals and the species at large. Human Existential Liberty is that definition, which, here, means: the degree with which a person or peoples possess the capacity to dictate the conditions and the course of their own existence. This is the central value of the ideological frame. To choose SobAlt earnestly is to choose to protect and expand the Existential Liberties of humans and humanity at large. The functionality and fitness of this Existential Liberty, as the central value of this ideology, is predicated on three major conditions.

First and most essential to establish is that liberty is not license. The distinction between liberty and license is one predicated on the presence or absence of considered responsibility and accountability to others. To possess liberty is not to possess license to do wrong onto others or so deprive them of their own liberties. There are two critical exceptions to this rule. First, is in defense of an offender. One can be justified in taking license with the liberties of another if that other person has taken license with the liberties of other people—think, sending a rapist to jail. This is the necessary concession societies make to uphold the institutions of justice. Next and last, is sacrificing liberty in the pursuit of species or societal continuity—think, the US draft in WWII: "Fight or your children will speak German."

Fittingly, the second major condition (although it's rather more of a prerequisite) of Human Existential Liberty serving as the central value of SobAlt is, human life and continuity. The truest and most complete loss of Human Existential Liberty would be our total reduction as a species. Either from extinction or the collapse of civilization, our Existential Liberties can perish; we can fail. As such, we must always strive to protect our futures against these great thieves of all we have and can yet achieve. If all be made shadowed by some great threat, if the breadth of our children grows uncertain, we must turn to our continuity above all else, for should we fail to deliver life or civilization to our unborn and unmade, we, too, will fail to return to them, to ourselves, the liberties sacrificed of our preservation. Human Existential Liberties cannot be made in the absence of human life or civilization. Continuity is paramount.

Before we move onto the last condition, and in light of the recent COVID-19 pandemic, it is necessary to provide a few moderating words on what qualifies as existential risk. In the early days of the pandemic, when information was short and many in the scientific community expected the worst, there was justification for things such as lockdowns and other infringements on individual liberties. It was truly uncertain whether this new disease was capable of threatening civilizational continuity, and we all must give allowance for that, but as more information emerged on the nature of the diseases, it became fairly obvious that while capable of inflicting great tragedy, COVID-19 was very likely incapable of inflicting apocalypse or even collapse. From our now privileged position of hindsight, it is clear that many of the responses to this incident took a disproportionate tithe on individual liberties as a result of sluggish adaptation to new information and poor communication. While not overly problematic in many Western nations, the pattern of decimating individual liberties under the pretext of "fighting COVID" seemed to be greatly exaggerated in nations with governments already leaning toward the authoritarian, in many cases serving only to compound tragedy[7,8]. Understand that justifying any reduction of liberty on the pretext of existential risk must be taken with the strictest scrutiny and demonstrate a clear, present, and severe risk to human and/or civilizational continuity.

Finally, the third major condition for Human Existential Liberty serving as the central value of SobAlt is its utility in informing examination and action for the three levels of analysis most central to a Humanist frame: that of the individual, the community, and the species as a whole.

At the individual level, Existential Liberty is perhaps most easily analyzed and understood. If you free a person from a failing organ, the crushing inexorability of a flood path, the chains of addiction, or financial destitution, you have given them a greater degree of freedom and agency with which to direct the course of their own life. The critical detail here is that you, the bringer of greater self-determination, do not seek to tell another what to do with their newfound freedom. There have been many attempts to collectively define what the pursuit of goodness and happiness should be for all individuals in a society. This is perhaps the core of the utopian fallacy. To assume that a single vision permeates or, perhaps worse, should permeate the dreams and desires of all peoples when, in truth, all of us seek different conditions and prizes of life. Where the Stalinists told the people, "Do not pray and work as I tell you, and I will bring you salvation," the sober Humanist must say, "Pray as you will, work as you will, and here are the tools to pursue your own dreams and aspirations." The beautiful, messy reality of us is that we are not all the same. One man's boring life is another man's paradise. Thus, the Sober Altruist must seek to expand the individual's capacity to dictate the conditions and course of their own existence, to deliver the means but not to dictate the ends.

The next essential level of analysis is that of community, which, in this book, describes any group of people that could be reasonably described as such, from a small school, a recreational club, or a country at large. The community's place in this ideological frame is defined foremost by its relationship to the individual. Communities are the ships upon which we build our lives and so define, in no small part, the liberties and bondages for the people within them. Mediating the symbiotic yet sometimes difficult, and sometimes even violent, relationship between a community and the individual (whether as a member of said community or otherwise) is essential to any earnest discussion on the boundaries and limits of Existential Liberty. This relationship is discussed several times in later chapters of this book.

Finally, but perhaps most abstract, is the value of Human Existential Liberty as applied to the species as a whole. It is estimated that at one point in our distant past, some seventy thousand years ago, we nearly went extinct. Less than ten thousand of us left on the planet[9], teetering on the edge of oblivion, of our future never happening at all. Just as so for those ten thousand, and for every subsequent generation, we are the shoulders upon which the peoples of the future stand, fall, or will never be at all. Those countless generations before won us elevation from the predations of night and lessened the lethality of scarcity; it is upon their shoulders that we stand as we are today. Similarly, our contributions to human continuity, elevations from scarcity, scientific discovery, and cultural enlightenments are our gifts to the species. These are how we blunt the limitations of mortality and elevate ourselves beyond the complete submission to the horrors and dictations of reality. A useful exercise to clarify this intergenerational and uniquely human quality is to look to the animal kingdom for comparison. For example, when a shark is born, there are no books to help it make sense of the world or technologies to make subsistence easier. When a shark is born, it starts from zero, a member of a species doomed to rediscover the beauty and horrors of the world for the first time with every newborn pup, and it has been so for the last 450 million years and counting[10]. When a new human is thrown into the world, it is not thrown without mooring, knowledge, or technology. This new person need not rediscover mathematics or the means of proper wound disinfection. This person does not start their struggles for being or understanding at zero; they start from where those who came before left off. Just as those before us gifted the tools to better shape our own existence, we must work to improve and pass along those tools to the next to carve the human story.

These three levels of analysis (the individual, the community, and the species) comprise a sort of ethical Russian nesting doll, wherein no one level can be truly analyzed separately as they are all pieces of a contextual whole, concluding but also beginning at the Existential Liberty of the individual. The will to generate human communities that prioritize the Existential Liberties of individuals allows for a world of diverse beliefs and traditions, but for such a world to manifest and endure, it must also demand of the individual a belief in the values that protect and expand those liberties. If you believe in nothing else, believe in this: Protecting and expanding the ability for humans to self-determine is an end worth fighting for, a value worth holding.

We'll conclude this chapter with a quote by Horace Mann from 1859[14], recently popularized by Neil Degrass Tyson, "Be ashamed to die until you have won some victory for humanity."

A SOBALT CRITIQUE OF
CONTEMPORARY LIBERTARIANISM:

米

This chapter will elucidate a brief critique of Libertarianism from our Humanist frame. In chapters one and two, we established that Human Existential Liberty is the guiding principle for the Sober Altruist, the central value of our ideology frame. Human Existential Liberty is here defined as the degree with which a person or peoples possess the capacity to dictate the conditions and course of their own existence. It then stands to reason that this Humanist ideology may have elements in common with another ideology for which liberty is similarly central. While this assumption is partially correct, where there are differences, they are stark.

Perhaps the easiest place to start is with a definition of Libertarianism. Libertarianism is a political philosophy that advocates only minimal state intervention in the free market and the private lives of citizens[11]. Several variations on this definition can be found, but two primary ideas typically underpin them. First, is that Libertarianism prioritizes individual liberty over essentially all else, and second, Libertarianism seeks to maximize individual liberty by minimizing the power and influence of the state (quick note here: "The state" has largely become shorthand for any institution capable of taking license with individual liberty unwillingly, that is to say, not just a government). This definition, though rightly centered around maximizing individual liberty, very commonly omits other sources of that which stunt our ability to self-determine.

It is so, in this dogged focus on the power of the state, that we will level our first critique. The state, though capable of inflicting great maladies on life and liberty, is far from the only source of injury upon the liberties of the individual. We are all born subject to the whims and malice of a reality that is indifferent to us at best and overtly hostile at worst. Who among us has not lost a loved one to sickness, addiction, scarcity, or disaster? We all have, and while some of these tragedies can be rightly, if only partially, attributed to the mismanagement of state or other institutions, many more cannot. The simple, brutal reality is that despite our present elevation from the worst of the world, we are at the whims of our environment, of circumstances imposed upon us by our bodies or by the very nature that bore them. The state may indeed bind you with chains and threats, but reality will do just the same with cancers and disaster. The means, the cause, and the degree of personal responsibility and influence are different but just as being falsely imprisoned can decimate the ability of a person to self-determine, so, too, can cancer consume your life and take from you control and agency. The Libertarian focus on limiting the power of the state to maximize the liberty of the individual omits the bondages forced upon us by all other sources. Pursuing liberty is not enough if liberty is defined solely as the absence of institutional encroachments on personal freedoms. Herein is where this Humanist doctrine diverges most starkly from Libertarianism and, so, brings us to our second critique. To blunt the bondages of reality and so expand Human Existential Liberty, strong institutions are and have always been essential. What's more is the role of strong institutions in civilizational continuity. A society predicated on the liberation of the individual via the disembowelment and castration of its institutions will lack the cohesion, morale, and organizational capacity necessary to avoid the predations of other societies seeking to subjugate and expand. Generating human communities that prioritize the Existential Liberties of the individual allows for a society of great freedom, but for such a society to manifest and endure, it must also demand of those within to contribute to its great engines of fortification and advance. Free societies need strong institutions to defend and expand that freedom.

To be clear, though, strong does not mean tyrannical; it means capable. A good illustration of this might be the infrastructure we use to travel. While far from perfect, the roads and rails we use every day grant us historically unprecedented access to our world. They even save lives by making emergency transport swift. Both public and private interests have worked together to bring us this freedom of movement. They have organized people and resources to accomplish something well beyond the ability of the individual. This is the vital utility of institutions. If the species is to endure and advance, it will be upon the backs of individuals organizing and cooperating through strong institutions, capable of moving us into the future and protecting the liberties we have now.

The final critique is aimed at a common Libertarian trope, the notion that all people should be free to use whatever drugs they'd like. This position highlights the unwillingness of our straw-manned Libertarian to intercede on personal freedoms even when that intersession will deliver the individual a greater capacity to self-determine. The position, simply stated, is thus: The state will not bind you by making certain drugs illegal; as such, you are free to sell yourself into chemical slavery. This is quite the oxymoron, quite the failure of governance. To remove restrictions on certain substances in favor of personal freedom ultimately destroys that personal freedom. The addictive nature of certain chemicals subverts rationality, and many who partake in these drugs know what they are doing costs them their ability to self-determine. Libertarianism may remove shackles, but it, too, removes the guardrails. Institutions (when not corrupted or degenerate) are essential to protect and maximize the ability of individuals to self-determine.

While drugs are perhaps the most obvious example of this critique, there are much more prolific and yet subtle ones like social media, for example, let's pick TikTok in particular. This app has been proven to be an intelligence-gathering platform for the Chinese Communist Party, a political body that holds beliefs and values that are simply anathema to the value of individual liberty. What's perhaps more disturbing is what TikTok is doing to the minds of our young. Numerous studies have demonstrated that this socially engineered software wreaks havoc on the mental well-being of the young user[12]. What's more is that it's demonstrably altering our cognitive functions, shortening attention spans and promoting addictive tendencies[12]. This is no accident. The Chinese equivalent of TikTok, Douyin, promotes educational videos and has strict time limits for younger users[13]. It does not promote vapid dances or whiney deconstructionists bent on hating the world they have been gifted. No, Douyin promotes science, skilled labor, and nationalism. What should this tell you? It should tell you that the CCP and the Chinese developers of TikTok know their platform is dangerous and are using it not only as a massive intelligence-gathering platform but also as a tool to weaken the morale of their enemies and pollute their youth. There have been several attempts to ban TikTok around the world, and some of them have been successful, though not nearly enough. The difficult question becomes, should a liberal society move to limit access to something like TikTok when we know it is damaging our children? When we know it is a spear aimed at bleeding the morale of the free world, is damaging the minds of our people, and is a weapon being used against us? Civilizations predicated on maximizing the liberty of the individual must draw the line and reject those things that threaten their values and continuity, or they will fall to the corrupting predations of authoritarian systems. Libertarianism, if ever applied as the driving political philosophy of a civilization, will neither serve to preserve that civilization nor preserve itself to be a passing fancy of the edgy anti-institutionalist.

We'll end this critique here with perhaps a cliche quote, an American idiom that can be found, among other places, carved into the somber black marble of the Korean War Memorial in Washington, DC[15]. "Freedom is not free."

THE HUMAN RELATIONSHIP WITH TECHNOLOGY AND THE PRECIPICE

※

This chapter will address a rather broad topic through the lens of our Humanist frame. As a recap, we established in chapters one and two that Human Existential Liberty is the guiding principle for the sober Humanist, the central value of our ideology frame. Human Existential Liberty is here defined as the degree with which a person or peoples possess the capacity to dictate the conditions and course of their own existence. Technology has been, and will always be, one of the foremost forces in shaping the trajectory of the species, but its value and function in our civilization has always been one of grim duality. Technology is perhaps the supporting character in the story of our long history, a force that we cultivate and foster and have always had a complicated relationship with. This relationship has never been more important or less constrained.

Since the decades preceding the Industrial Revolution, it's fair to say that we have been leaping like thrill-seeking children from one technological brink to the next. Jumping from industrialized warfare to mass production to self-annihilation—given form in nuclear arsenals—to many more such precarious ledges. There is a growing sense in our world, a growing weariness spawned by the recognition that as the rate of technological advance escalates, we will find ourselves at this brink more and more often. If you were born just thirty years ago, you have lived through the rise of the internet and the radical societal changes it has brought, the creation of personal computers, human genome mapping, GPS, GMOs, and renewable energy technologies, just to name a few. One of the stranger realities of the modern human experience is braving multiple and widespread changes to civilization as a result of the breakneck pace of technological advancements, all in a single lifetime. This rapidity of technological advance has translated to a rapidity in societal change. There has never been a time such as this, when our wisdom has been more thoroughly outmatched by the tools and technologies at our disposal. Never has there been a time in human history when a sober stance on technology and its place in our world has been more essential and more consequential to the human future. How we interact and treat our relationship with technology is likely to be the deciding factor in shaping the character of humanity in the years or, hopefully, millennia to come.

So, what, then, is the proper lens through which we should consider our relationship to technology? The sober and Humanist stance on technology is one that fundamentally relies on a reframing of what qualifies as human technological advance. There is a certain assumption in the modern world that all technology, when improved or conceived, constitutes an advance. SobAlt challenges that assumption. Say, next year, an ANI (artificial narrow intelligence) is created and given the keys to social media platforms. It masterfully manipulates users into using the platform more and ultimately makes them cognitive slaves to the app, programmed to orient their life toward this consumerist owner, even yanking at the proverbial leash. Another example: Nuclear weapons are made so devastating that a single launch could doom humanity as it sends the climate into apocalyptic disorder. Another, a chip is produced that can be injected into an individual and track various biomarkers and signals. Thirty years after its creation, it has been so thoroughly incorporated into the daily workings of society that the government, on the pretext of equity, elects to pay for the implanting of citizens and makes it illegal to forgo the procedure, and in so doing, ensures state access to an ultimate surveillance system. Last, an AGI (artificial general intelligence) rises to subtle control of the species, enslaving some while letting the rest die off. While some of these scenarios seem closer to science fiction, some are already here, and none of them (on a technological level at least) might be more than a few short decades away. Would anyone qualify a technology that results in the individual becoming a slave as "human technological advance"? Would you qualify the development of a weapon so technologically potent that a single accident could doom the world as "human technological advance"? Of course, the literary mechanism holds. A nuke of a higher yield is literally a more advanced nuke, but this is the common understanding of what constitutes technological advance, not one bound by its consequences or relationship with the human species.

The SobAlt must consider technology in context. We must consider technology more so by our relationship to it than by the face value and capability of the technology itself. If a technology does not deliver to us or otherwise grossly deprives us of our Existential Liberties, it is not human technological advance. At face, this Humanist orientation toward technology provides a clear position. Technological advance is qualified only by its contribution to Human Existential Liberties, but in practice, it is much more nuanced. This, of course, is due to the inherent duality of technology and indeed humanity itself. A good illustration of this duality is the combustion engine, which provides us with a freedom of movement that is historically unprecedented and connects our world in unfathomably consequential ways. It is the fiery, beating heart of a logistics system that fuels the modern world, saves remotes or overpopulated areas from starvation, allows us to see our families easily and often, and so much more. The combustion engine is (without a comparable replacement) an indispensable source of our contemporary and unprecedented freedom of movement. It is also the mechanism that powered the tanks of the Wehrmacht Blitzkrieg into Poland, the artificial winds upon which the warplanes of Russia bombed Georgia and most recently Ukraine, and upon which the US brutally bombed the Japanese islands in WWII. Whether or not these applications of violence were justified is not a point of consequence for these examples. What is of consequence is what they demonstrate. Technologies cannot be blanketly categorized as good or bad; rather, their applications, design intents, and specific manifestations must be the focus of our scrutiny. The internet is perhaps the most relevant example of this. It has provided ordinary people with extraordinary access to others and information, but it has also given rise to social media applications that actively and demonstrably harm and blunt the minds of our young[12, 13]. The internet is not bad, but there are ways of using it that clearly are.

In light of this Humanist orientation toward technology, there are two primary calls to action that must be illuminated.

First and most essential, is that of personal responsibility. There are few who walk in this world today who give serious thought to the technologies they embrace and those they should reject, despite this self-dialogue being an essential one in our era. While it is easy to proclaim that you have forgone a certain social media platform or to say, "I walk everywhere," it is harder to say that you have taken an earnest look into the technologies you allow into your life. Think. Do you participate in forms of entertainment that knowingly prey upon and manipulate the dopamine cycle? Do you allow corporations virtually unlimited access to personal information for the sake of convenience? Do you use technology to enable avoidance behaviors? Are you even capable of self-sufficiency without technologically enabled conveniences? These are not comfortable questions to answer. You may even come to answer them and concede. In the case of allowing corporations access to personal information, it may be, occasionally, worth allowing. There are tools that some, understandably, feel are powerful enough to justify a loss of privacy. What is harder to accept, harder to rationalize, is the reality that many of us have outsourced and so have allowed to atrophy the basic skills that have allowed us such things as food, warmth, community, and social or romantic connection. The sacrifice of these fundamental and essential skills for the sake of convenience is one of the steepest costs levied by accepting technologies recklessly and without review or moderation. Everyone must come to contend with these uncomfortable realities, these uncomfortable questions.

The conclusions people might draw from their self-dialogues on the technologies they allow into their lives will be different for everyone, but the point is to have them. To sell your liberty and privacy with scrutiny and intent rather than without question, comprehension, or healthy suspicion. It is easy to forget that if you are not paying for a service, you are not the customer. You are the product, or at least access to you is. There will always be platforms and services that would like nothing more than for you to sell them your attention or to have them perform some inconvenient task for the small price of personal data. It is first and foremost your responsibility to ensure that you partake in this era of wonder and plenty with awareness and caution, to ensure that you do not blunt the freeness of your mind or time by opening your arms to predatory technologies. Practicing regular self-reflection and, therefore, self-protection will only grow more essential as we continue to plummet into the technological unknown. In short, partake in the bounty of our technological wonders freely and enjoy them, but do not let them rule you.

The second call to action is perhaps a more difficult one as it requires a degree of civic engagement. There are technologies that possess the power to change the course of the human future, and we must engage with them earnestly. They will be the pillars of our further elevation from the cruelties of reality or the shovels we will remember as those that buried us under the weight of our machinations, greed, and arrogance. How this engagement must look will depend on one's country of residence, but a telling example hails from the United States. The Office of Technological Assessment, or OTA, was an office of the United States Congress that operated from 1974 to 1995[16]. The OTA's purpose was to provide congressional members and committees with objective and authoritative analysis of complex scientific and technical issues. Over the course of its twenty-one-year lifespan, the Office of Technological Assessment conducted nearly 750 separate assessments. It allowed for the mechanisms of government to engage with emerging technologies in an understandable way that was measured and thus allowed for value-based discussion to be had. While the OTA was certainly not the pinnacle of human technological skepticism, it did go a long way in promoting the notion that new technologies must be scrutinized and considered rather than casually allowed or casually investigated. Unfortunately, the OTA no longer exists, an absence that stands testament to our over-valuing of blind technological advance without care toward its wisdom or folly, its help or its harm. Another body called the Government Accountability Office, or the GOA, has stepped in to fill this void, although its efforts are not solely focused on technological assessments[17]. The course of action for the Sober American Altruist is clear: Engage with the mechanisms of government and advocate for the revival of the OTA or something similar. Lobby for a buffer between our technological capabilities and our cultures' failing wisdom. Do what it takes to get the institutions of power to ask, with authority, Should we? Not just, Can we? But why should anyone care? Why should anyone heed this call to action?

There will almost certainly be technologies that emerge in the next thirty years, perhaps even the next ten, that will possess abilities capable of threatening civilizational continuity, if only they are so applied or perhaps more concerningly, so unknowingly applied. There is no degree of self-abstinence from technology that can free a person from the tragedies of apocalypse or absolute tyranny, no shelter in this but for us all or for us none. Technologies such as AI and quantum computers will change the face of our world. We must be ready for this and face these challenges with values that prioritize humans and our agencies. In our hands, the hands of the living, rest the tools to protect ourselves and our future or the tools that will fail in their defense. The Sober Altruist must be vigilant, and our vigil must stand, for if we fail in its service, one eager leap or the next will prove our doom.

While perhaps grimly intriguing to consider the harms of technology, we cannot forsake or ignore the incalculable good it has and will continue to do for us. As much as it is necessary to guard ourselves against the worst of our own creations, we must foster the best of them. We must sharpen ourselves toward the greater mastery of our world, our future, and ourselves. If we fail in our balance and so come to reject technology, we will fail to outpace our world's inexorable entropic decline into sickness, famine, ignorance, and death. If we do not pursue those things that free us from our corporal bonds, we may never live to seek vital continuity amongst the stars, nor will our great-grandchildren live to see a world of plenty and choice.

It is ours, the living's obligation to foster the future and protect it against the great thieves of stagnation and excess; it is ours to take vigil.

SOBALT, THE WAY OF ACTION

$$\underset{\diagdown}{\overset{\diagup}{\ast}}$$

This chapter is perhaps the most essential as it explores Sober Altruism as the way of action and, so, the assumption of cause and responsibility. In previous chapters, we established that the goal of the SobAlt should be the expansion and protection of Human Existential Liberties. It is only through action that this conviction can be made manifest and that we might contribute ourselves to the human endeavor.

So often does it seem, especially among the secular, that people of our era want for nothing more deeply than they want for purpose, and yet still so often fail to find it. This is a search that persists despite a world filled with pain, hardship, broken people, and an uncertain human future. This blindness, this unwillingness to seek and assume responsibility, is a kind of living death, a tragic waste of the human birthright, a squandering of happiness and meaning, and the consuming embrace of only fleeting hedonistic relief. Purpose is everywhere. This chapter will explore how to find it, how to assume the responsibilities of SobAlt, and, so, become a scion of the human endeavor. There are two fundamental understandings we must come to before we can explore what that means in practice.

The first essential understanding of the nature of action is in how we comprehend its effects and consequences. The human perspective of time and chains of causality (of cause and effect) is extremely limited. None of us can predict the future with any degree of certainty or propose that our actions will never cascade into causing harm hundreds of years in the future. In the absence of that omnipotence, we are left with two tools with which to guide our own actions. A fallible but essential assessment of our potential impacts the historically speaking short-term, and more importantly, a precisely defined will toward acting with good intent. We've all heard the old adage, "The road to hell is paved with good intentions," and while certainly sometimes true, it is so often in our definition (or perhaps lack of definition) of what is "good" that we find ourselves led astray. Good intent is the intent to deliver people a greater capacity to self-determine. It is freeing people from their bindings so they might pursue their own dreams and aspirations. Good intent is looking to human continuity and to the Existential Liberties of those whom our great-grandchildren might call friends but whom we ourselves may never know.

The second and perhaps most essential understanding of the nature of action is an understanding of the human birthright. Our genesis, our awakening into a biological and self-aware species, inherently grants us purpose and meaning. Should we instead have appeared without our bodies, as floating consciousness, non-corporeal, generated from nothing and without history, undying, never hungry, tired, or able to feel, what purpose could we then have? Our membership, our very bones and biology, the vessels we are, the vessels of our mothers and fathers and their parents before them, are the inheritance of our hopes, love, compassion, pain, struggles, meaning, and our purpose. Hollow it would be to appear as such a floating thing. Yet we do not; our birthrights are meaning and purpose, crowned upon us as our very flesh and bone. Like all great crowns, ours do not come without responsibility or imperative nor without cost. It is through action that we choose to don this crown, and through action that we pay our tithes to it. To live bearing the standard of SobAlt is to accept the crown of blood and bone and do what you can while you are here.

Armed with these two understandings, we can take action with decisiveness, care, and intent. There are two arenas, two types of action that the SobAlt must pursue. First, is the act of self-emancipation or the act of self-care and construction. Second, is that of action for others.

Consider that old adage, the maxim of first responders and rescuers alike, "Save yourself before you save anyone else." This at first seems to fly in the face of what it means to be a SobAlt. Even the definition of altruism seems to stand in stark relief to this dogma, but this could not be further from the truth. The reason this adage has endured in the circles of our boldest and bravest is because it is wholly pragmatic in its process and approach to coming to the aid of others. Its simple truth rings clear in the extremis from which it was born but also in the mundane. It is difficult, if not impossible, to help others in a meaningful way if you are helpless or in need of rescuing. There are essential liberties that we all must cultivate for ourselves such that we might have the freedom to help others and the strength to carry some small part of the human future. These freedoms are not complex, nor do they require extravagance to achieve. We'll take a moment to describe the most essential five of these personal freedoms but understand that there are many more.

First, is a sufficient and sustainable elevation from privation or material insecurity. For most of us, this means pursuing a career that will grant us financial stability, but for all of us, this means careful planning and attention to the affairs of household, personal wealth, and financial freedoms. SobAlts should also pursue a degree of material preparedness. Whether that be extra foodstuffs in the basement as the Mormons do or cultivating skills such as hunting, fishing, and gardening, we must be able to rely on ourselves before others can rely on us, even and especially in extreme circumstances. These securities allow us our base and ensure that our basic needs are met. Again, this does not particularly require extravagance; it only requires a degree of material comfort sufficient to meet our basic needs and, more importantly, allow us the space for altruism and additional responsibilities.

Second, is health. This should not be a surprise. Our vessels, though magnificent, have flaws and require a great deal of care and attention. There are few greater losses of agency a person can endure than to have their body fail and drag them into sickness and decay. Of course, we will all die, but to maximize the good we are able to do, we should strive to build of our bodies bastions that will endure time and hardship. The way we choose to treat our bodies is no less than a reflection of our reverence for our ancestors who passed them to us. It reflects the seriousness with which we treat our responsibilities to kith and kin and the conviction with which we hold toward a better future. Our bodies are a reflection of our dedication to others, ourselves, and indeed, our species. Your potential for goodness and kindness, for contribution and family, for thought and noble suffering is universally worth living for, and thus, worth growing old for. Care for yourself as if you are the sum of all the goodness that has and might yet come from your life. Care for yourself as you would care for the people who already love and rely on you and those who may yet do so. Care for yourself so you can care for others with longevity and worth.

Third, is education, or perhaps more precisely, freedom from ignorance. To evict ignorance is to inform action with greater effect and, so, pursue our Existential Liberties with greater efficacy. Acumen is the foundational guide for all other ethics of action as it is in our comprehension of reality and the accuracy of that understanding that we might find ways to improve ourselves and our world. The SobAlt must seek to learn from all sources and should not presume to dismiss any works of humanity, especially religious ones, as they are vital to pursuing complete histories in ethics, law, literature, philosophy, human experience, and governance. Consume ideas, ponder philosophies, embrace nuisance, come to know our history with intimacy, but foremost, strive to think critically and defy ignorance wherever you might find it. The cultivation of ourselves in knowledge is an antidote to our mortal limitations, for in learning, we expand ourselves beyond the bounds of brevity and singularity so we might come to know the wisdom born of billions across the paradigms of millennia. Never has the privilege of knowledge been so free, and yet, it is still only a privilege for those who make it one.

Four. Discipline is a great freedom, a truth familiar in its loving plagiarism through millennia of thought. As we seek greater Existential Liberties for ourselves and others and so seek elevation from the bondages of the external world, we must also cultivate a freedom from self, a freedom from our internal worlds. Strive to master skills that allow you control over emotion, vice, and all else that might make you dull.

Seek to manifest only those things wished and not dismissed by pragmatism. Purge that which brings reward-less chaos and might take from you agency. We are both smith and implement forged. We must strive to know best the art of crafting and maintaining ourselves. We cannot hope to rule our future or contribute meaningfully if we are forged or kept weakly and, so, bent as slaves to every passing want and whim. There is no more fundamental tool than that of oneself and no more fundamental skill than its mastery. In our age of overwhelming distraction, excess, and vapidity, there is perhaps no greater personal victory than to keep ourselves from their temptations and stagnating influences.

Five, is building and maintaining community. Few elements of the human condition have granted us more advantage over our world than our social nature, yet also, few elements of the human condition can bring us more harm and hardship than denying those same social proclivities. Despite how it may seem when we are young and coddled in the social envelope of our childhood, building community doesn't just happen. It takes dedication, intent, and effort. There are so many ways to build community in our age; there are groups spanning every conceivable interest and that organize in-person events through social media platforms. There are community centers and gyms, modern-day temples of service and self-improvement. There are spiritual centers and churches. There is no excuse for not seeking and building community around you, just as there is no excuse for contenting yourself with digital communities alone. Get to know your neighbors, seek connections in the places you frequent, spend time creating community with the time you might have otherwise spent escaping into the digital world. None of us can or should have to face the challenges and frequently harsh realities of our existence alone. We need each other; neglect that truism at your peril[5].

As stated previously, these five personal freedoms are not remotely inclusive of all the things we should be seeking for ourselves, but they are the most foundational and, so, the most critical. With these five, we are best able to direct our attention outward and truly become a scion of the human endeavor. There are two critical modes of engagement, or categories of action, that must be pursued in this way. They are: obligations and missions.

Obligations are, as the title suggests, actions that we all must take. The nature of your obligations might differ from community to community or country to country, but they are largely universal. Here, again, we will explore the most essential three, but these are by no means all-encompassing.

Perhaps our most essential obligation is the one we have toward the communities and indeed, the civilizations that bear us. Our freedoms to make of this life what we wish are largely defined by our communities and countries. It is our obligation to uphold these things, to contribute to their continuity and prosperity and give ourselves to the service of our institutions and our communities. There are so many who live their lives consumed by their own ends or miseries, content only with leaching upon the body politic without ever an aim to protect it or repay it in service. It is difficult to imagine a higher degree of apathy or unworthiness to the gifts of humanity than to imagine someone who understands, as we all do in this age, the trials and sacrifices it takes to hold our civilizations together, and yet still does not wish to contribute, to sacrifice for its gifts and privileges. It is not a herculean act to fulfill your obligations to your country and community. It is only earnest civic engagement, service to others in whatever way you see your-self most suited for, and the understanding that everything we have is earned by people who sacrificed for something greater than themselves.

Part of this obligation we have to our communities and society is a kind of ongoing civilizational vetting. None of our communities or countries are perfect, and they never will be. It is our responsibility to draw the line, and if our institutions should cross those lines, should breach unimpeachable free-doms or neglect themselves in their defense, it is our respon-sibility to correct these maladies in whatever ways we must. Here, again, is the importance of earnest civic engagement, to prevent these things with words and politics before politics by other means becomes a grim necessity. SobAlt is inherently an institutionalist doctrine, but as much as that means the defense and guidance of critical institutions does it also mean their policing, scrutinizing, and if necessary, disassembly.

The second essential obligation, we have is family, chil-dren, and parenting. There are perhaps few other obligations so essential to the human experience and its successful conti-nuity than creating and rearing our young. Procreation and par-entage are the fundamental modes with which we persist, the manifestation of hope, youth infinite in potential and our very future incarnate. Such is a future that must be cultivated with intent and care, a future whose mechanisms must be protected and held as one of the penultimate responsibilities of the human experience. We must raise our young and raise them with pur-pose. In doing so, we might bring them up better than we are. Raise our youth in cultures and families that are responsible, stable, supportive, and invested in the future. We must seek to pass to the young the depths of human kindness, the history from which they spring, the privilege of their humanity and the imperatives of that privilege. We must nurture our young in the best ways circumstance makes possible and as shown in outcome. As grimly fatalistic as it sounds, there is a reason a significant percentage of incarcerated people in the US hail from fatherless homes[18]. There is a reason why two-parent households produce more successful offspring under a substantial spread of metrics[19]. Our responsibility in this is absolute, to wield the powers of generation and parentage as nothing less than the mechanisms of human expansion and continuity that they are. This by no means should encourage celibacy or sex only for the sake of procreation. Sex is an essential element of the human experience, one to be enjoyed but not done so too lightly. Rarely are we more directly responsible for the future or more able to shape its character than when we are responsible for the future of a child.

Third and last, is somewhat unique among its peers as it is as much of an acknowledgment as it is an obligation. There are at least two breeds of evil that lurk in the heart of man. There are people who intend evil and are rightly judged as monsters, and then there are people who intend well and are similarly and rightly judged as monsters. It is perhaps the most frightening reality of the human condition that ordinary people can be coerced into committing, ignoring, or condoning extraordinary evil. The arrogant will maintain that they are singularly immune to corrupting influence. To combat this stunning ignorance, one need only direct them to our recent history, when entire nations' worth of ordinary men and women became the mechanisms of the Holocaust, the purges of Mao's Great Leap Forward, or the many historically recent genocides of the indigenous. If there is one lesson you take from this book, let it be this: None of us are immune from a slow transformation into what history could remember as it remembers the Nazis or Stalinists. It is only through earnest self-reflection, intellectual courage, clear values, and the will to speak truth and stand against injustice that any of us can be secure in the knowledge we will not be remembered in infamy. Evil does exist in the hearts of men, the desire for dominion and wanton violence, to impose your will upon others and take license with their way of life or even their right to life. The values of SobAlt are clear, and as much as they are aimed at achieving a greater dominion for mankind over its circumstances, it is, too, aimed at ensuring that we do not become our own tyrants. If we are to take some small measure of responsibility for the human condition and its future, that effort must include the recognition of the evils that lurk in ourselves and the world around us and an earnest commitment to stand against them. A cloud asks not from where the wind blows, but clouds and people are held to different standards, as is the burden of sentience.

The final expression of action for the species is that of mission. This word, mission, is meant in much the same way as it is in our non-secular communities. None of us are omnipotent nor are our energies infinite. We cannot fight all battles, but we can fight a few with excellence and impact. Consider what those few battles might be to you and pursue them; make them your mission for the human endeavor. Meditate on this choice with great care for in it is a solemn declaration to meet your chosen mission with excellence and endurance. Each one of us might bring ourselves to different missions and for different reasons, but we must each share in action. From those who teach the young the skills of debate to those who guide the march of technology to those who secure the needs of an entire nation. These are all united in action, efforts that ripple in eternity. If you are passionate about education, educate in your community. If you have suffered from the throws of addiction, help others shed the yolk of chemical slavery. If you are politically minded, get involved! There is a world of need; you need only see it and commit yourself to its aid. No matter the scale or the cause, know that action is not humbled by our mortal scope, but rather, magnified through it onward. No action is too small nor effort unworthy. Consider how to ritualize this choice of mission, whether it be a letter to yourself, a promise to a loved one who has passed, or a tattoo, as examples. It is right to ritualize and wear the choice to endure our burdens willingly and with grace; it is right to make a reminder, a promise, to keep ourselves from neglecting ourselves, our mission, and our obligations to the world around us.

With this choice of mission must also come a caution to not become the author of stories not our own but instead provide others the keys to their own agency. In all actions taken for others, we must strive to deliver liberties over context, self, and environment but never ourselves become an impediment to the Existential Liberties of those we seek to aid. Consider actions that might help people become better masters of themselves and directors of their own existence. Free peoples from the shackles of ignorance, the chains of self-pity, or endemic frailty or lift them above the toxic dictations of toxic contexts. As we walk our chosen mission and so act upon it with intent and caution, we must also avoid temporal narrowness. We must know our own brevity and so recognize future generations and their efforts and struggles to come. Action for others cannot be relegated only to those who now live but also to those nameless billions whom we might never know yet for whom we are now responsible. Weigh action in the expanse of the human endeavor as, therein, action takes lasting effect.

To live bearing the standard of SobAlt is to meet our obligations to self and species. It is to choose a mission and bear its trials, successes, pains, and responsibilities. It is to expressly assume a burden to the human endeavor; whether that be carried in tragedy or victory, oblivion or peace, it is ever yours to bear.

In all modes of action, whether that be action for yourself or for others, we must act with severity and focus. It is so easy to fall astray and into the arms of distraction and inconsequence, to live a life devoid of authenticity and meaning. As our culture plummets ever further into the materialist reductionist hellscape that science fiction authors have been warning us about for decades, we must cling to our values such that we might avoid the meaningless distractions so lauded by those themselves who are empty and without cause.

We'll conclude this chapter with help from a quote from the Roman satirical poet Juvenal written circa 100 CE[20] "... Already long ago, from when we sold our vote to no man, the People have abdicated our duties; for the People who once upon a time handed out military command, high civil office, legions—everything, now restrains itself and anxiously hopes for just two things: bread and circuses." In our pursuit of the authentic and meaningful, of a better human future, we should hold one idea, one phrase in a place of significance in our minds. A phrase that embodies an earnest commitment to the authentic, to action and impact, and foremost, to the values of SobAlt: Spoil the Bread, Burn the Circus.

Death is a state separate from life and yet also separate from never having been at all, a state where cause may be at rest but effect ripples ever onward. Each, our ripples, carry us with all others to the end of ends, to truly cease only if our ripples, each and all, the tempest of humanity, should break against cliffs unwearable or so fade into placid stillness.

CONCLUSION

$\times\vert\angle$
$\diagup\vert\angle$

The question that remains is: Why? Why burden yourself with the weight of others or blister your feet in joining the march of human progress? There are, of course, the more selfish reasons already presented, such as meaning, direction, and conviction, but what else? If you are reading this, it is likely that you have lived a life of unimaginable comfort and agency compared to the vast majority of human history. It is likely that you have access to knowledge and resources in a way that people of our past simply did not. We are all thrown into the world without a choice of when, where, or to whom, and yet you, reader, what blessings or great luck did this apathetic toss of the universe grant you? Not being hunted by creatures of the dark or perishing in ignorance at the slightest mystery, nor rotting of an infection that simple antibiotics could heal. How, then, did you, like all of us denied a choice of place or time, find yourself here, now, in this time of relative plenty?

While none of us are given a choice as to the age or circumstance we are thrust into, those thrown before us do have a different choice, a hand in shaping our world. You, dear reader, rolled the dice of cosmic destiny, or chance, if you prefer, and landed here. Here, in this age of plenty and choice. Far from perfect, but it is not the green terror of the jungles of old nor swept by the arid breath of famine. For these gifts, we have ordinary men and women to thank. Although none of us have a choice in where or when our consciousness awakes, those who came before chose to build us something to help us on our journey, and so we contend with life supported and un-alone. The moment you understand that you, the thrown, are responsible, at least in part, for the conditions of those yet to be, is the moment you are culpable for the choice to ignore that responsibility or to accept the burdens of our future.

We tend to think of social contracts as agreements held between individuals and other elements of their societies, but this so often omits perhaps the most essential social contract a human can endorse: our perpetual contract with the dead and those yet to be. As none of us have a choice in where we awake into sentience, our best hope is in trusting that those who came before wished to build a better world for us to inhabit. As we know, this is not always the case but clearly happens often enough to bring us into our comparatively prosperous era. What we can ensure is that we will choose to uphold our contract with the dead and the unborn. In good faith and under the burdens of fallibility and our mortal limitations, we can choose to build a better world and uphold the perpetual contract of mankind and its obligations.

Despite our best efforts, there is so much of life we will never have a hand in choosing. We will all perish; will all suffer at the hands of events we cannot control and lose people we love. There may even come a day when the light of humanity fails, and we are remembered only by the ashes we leave behind. There are, however, things we can choose. We can choose to uphold our contract with the dead and unborn. We can choose to live with our backs to the last wall and fight for our continuity and future, not because there is some divine mandate to do so, a guarantee we can succeed in perpetuity, nor a promise of some grand reward when our burdens are done, but because it is right. Choose to fight because countless generations fought to bring you this far, and countless yet depend on you for every moment of existence and grace their lives might bring.

The hero's journey is a misunderstood thing in our age. Too many stories lie to us and whisper, "There has been no call to adventure for you, no wizard in a pointy hat knocking at your door, and so you must not be the hero, or at least not yet." Life is not like stories. Purpose doesn't knock on your door; you either find it or it will never find you. The world is starved for heroes, and the men and women capable of rising to that occasion are sitting at home waiting for a knock on their door that will never come. Meanwhile, our world hurdles into the unknown, burns of war and disaster, and our future has never been more unclear. So, if it must, let this be your call to adventure, the knock on your door. Our future is uncertain, the world is burning, and it needs you.

I cannot choose to live forever, nor deign to understand the secrets of the universe, but I can choose to do this:

I can choose to protect our continuity and future. To live with my back to the last wall not because I must but because somebody must. Our future must be guarded, the perpetual contract of mankind fulfilled. The vigil must stand.

SOBALT AND COMING TO A NAME

$\ast$

Throughout the decade-long process of articulating what I have come to call a doctrine of Sober Altruism, I have gone through several iterations of the name. These names have washed in and out of use in my personal writings, and truly, none of them have stuck. This book contains the first real attempt to share my ideas and, as those of you who have had the privilege of teaching will surely know, if you wish to deepen your understanding of something, prepare it in a format to be consumed by someone who knows nothing about it. As a consequence of this book, of this exercise in communication, I have come to decide on a name, a simple contraction of a phrase I already use, SobAlt, short, of course, for Sober Altruism. Now, I'm afraid I've rather rushed into the conclusion of this notation in its very first paragraph, but I think it's an interesting exercise, if only for me, to trace the other three names I have primarily known this doctrine by and explore a bit about how these names reflect an immaturity or unfinishedness of SobAlt during the times of their use.

The very first name I gave to this idea, or more accurately, the unfinished notion of this idea, was Autodiction. This conjunction of the Latin words for "self" and "narration" captured, though poorly, the central value of SobAlt; that is, the goal of the sober Humanist should be the expansion of individual agencies, of the human capacity to self-dictate or self-narrate the course and conditions of their existence. You'll notice I avoided using the word liberty in defining Autodiction, and that is because this first name predates the concise definition of SobAlt's aims as expanding and protecting Human Existential Liberties. Even the word "liberty" was wholly absent from earlier iterations of this doctrine as I simply had not considered that liberty could be made to encapsulate, precisely, the aims of Sober Altruism if only expressly broadened to include the sum of our existential realities. This name slowly faded from use as its connotations were not quite precise enough as I came to define the doctrine more completely.

The next name I used for quite a while, likely four to five years in total, and was another Latin phrase, albeit a real one this time rather than a forced conjunction. *Vexillum* is a Latin word that literally translates to "tiny sail". This word came to describe the war banners of ancient Rome, the standards under which the legions of Rome marched. The attraction to this name is not hard to imagine. A large part of the appeal, the draw of SobAlt, is its presentation of a secular moral direction, a standard by which we might judge the deeds and obligations of others and ourselves. This name, however, marked perhaps the darkest period in writing this doctrine as, for lack of a more accurate phrase, I self-radicalized toward the worst interpretations of SobAlt, unmoderated by the essentials of Kant or Aurelius or even the basics of the Western Ethos to live and let live. I tried, for a self-inflicted and foolish lack of alternative, to live in a reality of consequence alone, of justifying immorality in the present for what I felt was a glimpse of a better future. As is so often the case, curing my own philosophical and ethical ignorance cured my hate and allowed the more radical tendencies of the doctrine to moderate and yield to the unimpeachable virtues of individual liberty and acting on truly good intent. The warring origins of this name came to hold a sort of psychological scar for me. *Vexillum* came to represent the worst aspects of ideology, and indeed, myself, and so, I stopped using it.

The last name I came to was the shortest-lived but perhaps the best of the three I settled on before SobAlt. Human Existential Liberty, being the central value, the core of the doctrine, seemed like a natural place from which to derive a name, and so I did. I used the acronym HEL (Human Existent Liberty), which, of course—and regrettably—is pronounced hell. While at first, I felt this name suited its purpose, I came to realize that using it could be somewhat inflammatory and goad those more religious among us into conflict with SobAlt, which has never been and never will be my aim. I consider the contempt many Humanists have toward theists as a perfect demonstration of where traditional Humanism has utterly failed. There is nothing of SobAlt that attempts to disprove the divine or take faith from the faithful as the simple truth is, these two ideas are (with a few exceptions such as scriptural literalists) not inherently incompatible, and, more importantly, I have found that, generally speaking, those with clearly articulated belief structures, regardless of what those structures contain, have much more in common with each other than with those without an articulated belief structure at all. And so, again, HEL fell out of use in my writings.

I feel SobAlt is a suitable mix of preciseness and severity. It captures the necessity of altruism and the seriousness with which we must take our obligations without overtly alienating other people who might disagree; as after all, we are all just people.

To name a thing, makes a thing.

REFERENCES

[1] National Science Foundation (2009, March 5). "Evidence of Earliest Known Domestic Horses Found in Kazakhstan." National Science Foundation. https://www.nsf.gov/news/news_summ.jsp?cntn_id=114345#:~:text=Evidence%20of%20Earliest%20Known%20Domestic%20Horses%20Found%20in%20Kazakhstan,The%20use%20of&text=Evidence%20of%20thong%20bridle%20use,early%20as%205%2C500%20years%20ago

[2] Hawley, D. (2022, December 8). "History of the Invention of Cars." J.D. Power. https://www.jdpower.com/cars/shopping-guides/history-of-the-invention-of-cars

[3] Lyotard, J.-F. (1979). *The Postmodern Condition: A Report on Knowledge.* University of Minnesota Press.

[4] Wikipedia Contributors (n.d.). "Post-postmodernism." In Wikipedia. https://en.wikipedia.org/wiki/Post-postmodernism#cite_note-8

[5] Putnam, R.D. (2000). *Bowling Alone: The Collapse and Revival of American Community.* Simon & Schuster.

[6] American Humanist Association (n.d.). "Definition of Humanism." American Humanist Association.

https://americanHumanist.org/what-is-Humanism/definition-of-Humanism/#:~:text=Humanism%20is%20a%20philosophy%20of,to%20be%20of%20paramount%20importance

7. The British Academy. (2021). "COVID Decade: Understanding the Long-term Societal Impacts of COVID-19." The British Academy. https://www.thebritishacademy.ac.uk/documents/3238/COVID-decade-understanding-long-term-societal-impacts-COVID-19.pdf

8. Swart, M. (2020, March 12). "How the coronavirus has deepened human rights abuses in China." Al Jazeera. https://www.aljazeera.com/news/2020/3/12/how-the-coronavirus-has-deepened-human-rights-abuses-in-china

9. Krulwich, R. (2012, October 22). "How Human Beings Almost Vanished From Earth in 70,000 B.C." NPR. https://www.npr.org/sections/krulwich/2012/10/22/163397584/how-human-beings-almost-vanished-from-earth-in-70-000-b-c

10. Davis, J. (n.d.). "Shark evolution: A 450 million year timeline." Natural History Museum. https://www.nhm.ac.uk/discover/shark-evolution-a-450-million-year-timeline.html

11. Wikipedia Contributors (n.d.). "Libertarianism." In Wikipedia. https://en.wikipedia.org/wiki/Libertarianism

12. Depression and Bipolar Support Alliance. (n.d.). "TikTok and Youth Mental Health." Depression and Bipolar Support Alliance. https://www.dbsalliance.org/education/newsletters/tiktok-and-youth-mental-health

13. Van Boom, D. (2021, September 20). "TikTok's China equivalent limits kids to 40 minutes a day." CNET. https://www.cnet.com/culture/tiktoks-china-equivalent-limits-kids-to-40-minutes-a-day

14. Wikiquote Contributors (n.d.). "Horace Mann." In Wikiquote. https://en.wikiquote.org/wiki/Horace_Mann

15. Wikipedia Contributors (n.d.). "Freedom isn't free." In Wikipedia. https://en.wikipedia.org/wiki/Freedom_isn%27t_free

16. Wikipedia Contributors (2021, October 19). Office of Technology Assessment. In Wikipedia. https://en.wikipedia.org/wiki/Office_of_Technology_Assessment

17. U.S. Government Accountability Office (n.d.). "What GAO Does." U.S. Government Accountability Office. https://www.gao.gov/about/what-gao-does

18. Kofler-Westergren, B., Klopf, J. & Mitterauer, B. (2010). "Juvenile delinquency: Father absence, conduct disorder, and substance abuse as risk factor triad." *International Journal of Forensic Mental Health*, 9(1), 33–43. https://doi.org/10.1080/14999013.2010.483345

19. Wilcox, W. B. (2021, February 1). "Less Poverty, Less Prison, More College: What Two Parents Mean for Black and White Children." Institute for Family Studies. https://ifstudies.org/blog/less-poverty-less-prison-more-college-what-two-parents-mean-for-black-and-white-children

20. Wikipedia Contributors (2021, August 6). "Bread and circuses." In Wikipedia. https://en.wikipedia.org/wiki/Bread_and_circuses

21. Oxford English Dictionary, s.v. "sober, adj.", September 2023. https://doi.org/10.1093/OED/2287152955

22. Oxford English Dictionary, s.v. "altruism, n.", July 2023. https://doi.org/10.1093/OED/2655897841

23. Oxford English Dictionary, s.v. "ideology, n.", July 2023. https://doi.org/10.1093/OED/9578528666

ACKNOWLEDGMENTS

To Zach Foley: From long-time roommate at North Dakota State University to valued advisor for all of my endeavors, this could not have been done without your sound advice, reasonability and support. A person could not ask for a better friend. For this, I am forever grateful.

To the North Dakota State University (NDSU), Emergency Management Undergraduate and Graduate program and faculty: To all the faculty and staff who made my education in Emergency Management possible, thank you for your enduring commitment to excellence and your role in forging professionals capable of meeting the many challenges of our age. This project started in the walls of your lecture halls. Thank you all.

To Susie Schaefer: Thank you for your advice and patience throughout the process of publishing this personal obsession. I would have been lost in the process without you. Thank you.

59

ABOUT THE AUTHOR

V incent Burkhardt is a career Emergency Manager in the United States with extensive experience in disaster science and response in numerous sectors. Throughout his schooling and practice of Emergency Management, he sought to articulate the values underlying the field, the very human reasons we choose to cry out against the inevitable horrors and conditions of our reality. Over a ten-year obsession with this quest for articulation, he found answers to these questions rooted in the very heart of what it means to be human.

www.ingramcontent.com/pod-product-compliance
Lightning Source LLC
Chambersburg PA
CBHW022342280326
41934CB00006B/742

9798989359608